Prince Edward Island
Lighthouses
by Harold Stiver

Copyright Statement

Table of Contents

Tours

A Short History of Lighthouses

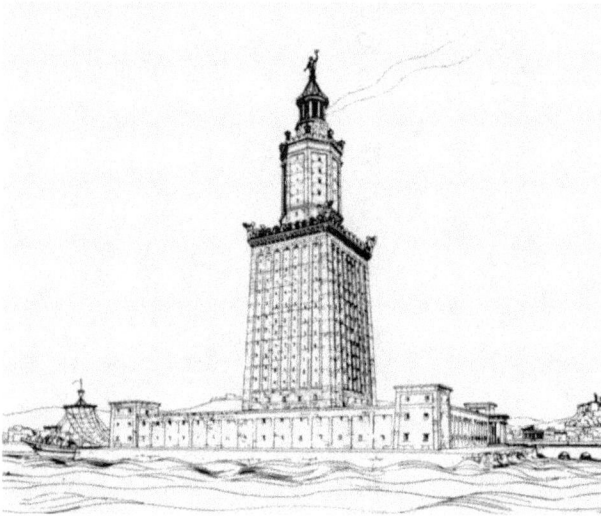

There is some evidence of a lighthouse from the 5th century B.C. of Themistocles of Athens constructing a stone column with a fire on top. This was at the harbour of Piraeus, associated with Athens.

However one of most famous and spectacular early structures was the Lighthouse of Alexandria, or the Pharos of Alexandria. It was one of the Seven Wonders of the Ancient World.

The lighthouse was built in the Third Century B.C. in Alexandria, Egypt by Ptolemy II. It stood on the island of Pharos in the harbour of Alexandria and was said to be 110 metres (350 feet) high.

The lighthouse was built in three stages, a large square at the bottom, an octagonal layer in the middle, and a cylindrical tower at the top.

The structure lasted until a series of earthquakes damaged it, with the 1303 Crete earthquake resulting in its destruction.

The Tower of Hercules, in northwest Spain, is modelled after the Pharos Lighthouse.

The first lighthouse in Canada was built in 1734 in Louisbourg on Cape Breton Island, Nova Scotia. Over the years, the structure was damaged beyond repair in a battle between the British and the French in 1758, destroyed by fire in 1923 and had to be rebuilt several times. The lighthouse known today was built in 1923.

Currently Canada's oldest surviving lighthouse is Sambro Island Lighthouse, built in 1758 at the entrance to Halifax Harbour. It is seen in the image above.

The oldest surviving lighthouse in Prince Edward Island is the Point Prim Lighthouse which was opened in 1845. It was built by Richard Walsh and designed by Isaac Smith.

The lighthouse is circular and made of brick, one of only two so built in Canada. The other is called Fisgard Lighthouse which is located in British Columbia. Point Prim Light Station is open every day (10am-6pm) from late June to early September.

Prince Edward Island County Map

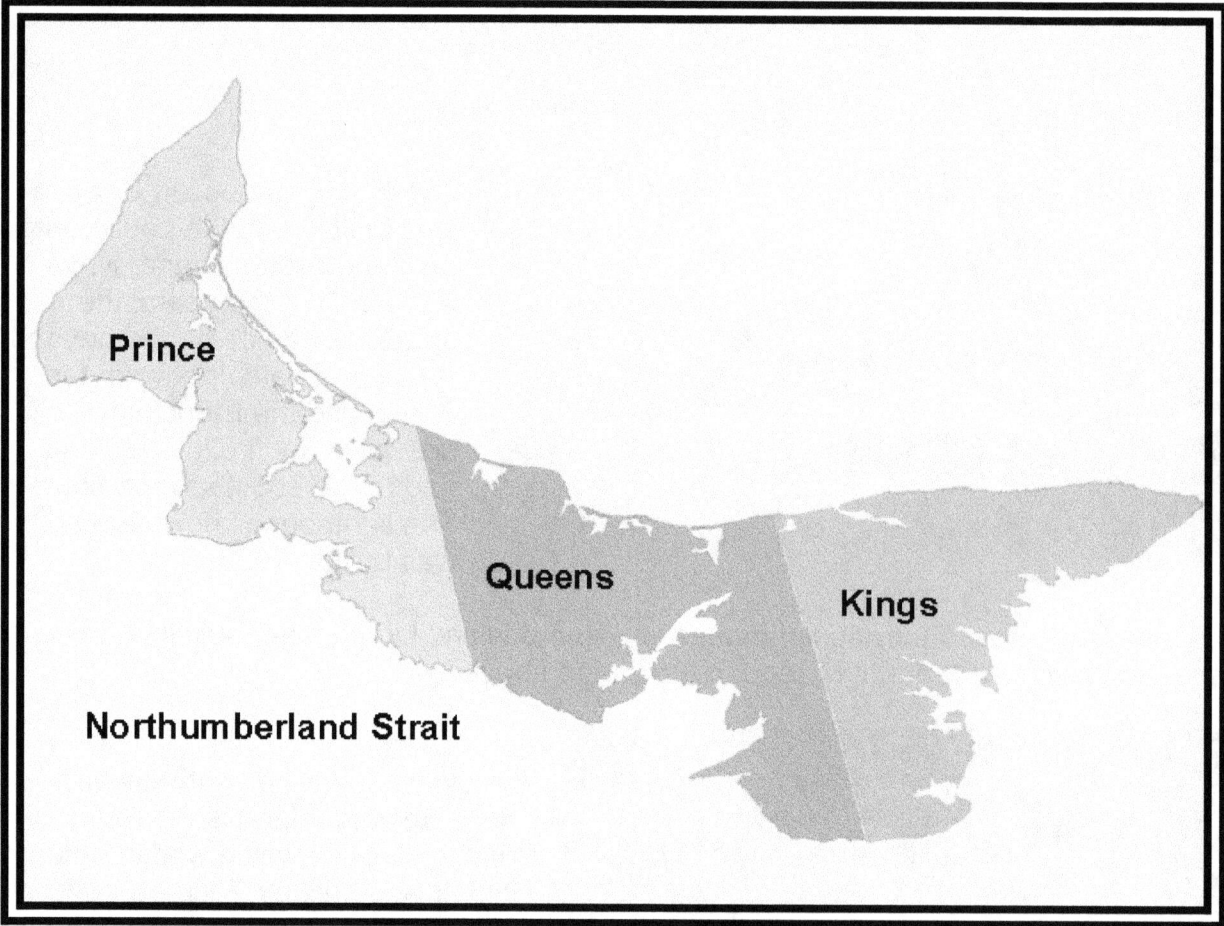

Prince

Queens

Kings

Northumberland Strait

Annandale Range Lighthouses

The Annandale Range Lighthouses were built in 1898 as an aid to ships travelling into Grand River and to the wharf at Annandale. The rear range light was destroyed in a gale in 1900 and the lights were shut off until a new tower was erected in 1905. This new tower is the tallest in Prince Edward Island. The rear tower was deactivated in 2015 and sold to private owners who have opened it as an overnight rental.

Front Range

Description: Square white pyramidal

Location: Annandale

Directions: From PE-310 west of Little Pond, head south on Annandale Wharf Rd for 1.9 km and the site

Coordinates: 46°15'33.0"N 62°25'20.0"W

Opened: 1898

Automated: 1964

Deactivated: 1990

Height: 5 meters, 17 feet

Focal Height: 9 meters, 31 feet

Signal: White flash every second

Visitor Access: Grounds and tower closed

Rear range (Image above)

Description: Square white pyramidal

Location: Annandale

Directions: From PE-310 west of Little Pond, head south on Nortons Rd 1.1 km and the site

Coordinates: 46°15'58.0"N 62°26'10.0"W

Opened: 1901

Automated: 1964

Deactivated: 2015

Height: 20 meters, 65 feet

Focal Height: 23 meters, 76 feet

Signal: White flash every 4 seconds

Visitor Access: Grounds and tower closed

Big Tignish Lighthouse

The Big Tignish Lighthouse was built in 1881 by Henry Williams as an aid to vessels entering the Tignish Harbour. It was deactivated in 1997 and was moved to Fisherman's Haven Community Park in 2009 as part of a seaside park.

Description: Square white pyramidal with black horizontal band

Location: Tignish Shore

Directions: 100 Tignish Run, Tignish Shore Rd

Coordinates: 46°56'44.8"N 63°59'39.9"W

Opened: 1881

Automated: 1962

Deactivated: 1997

Height: 8 meters, 27 feet

Focal Height: 11 meters, 35 feet

Signal: Fixed white

Foghorn signal: N/A

Visitor Access: Grounds open, tower closed

Blockhouse Point Lighthouse

The Blockhouse Point Lighthouse is the second oldest light station on the island. It was erected in 1876 by James W. Butcher to aid ships entering the Charlottetown Harbour. The lighting was upgraded in 1909 to a fourth-order Fresnel lens. The lighthouse was automated on July 25th, 1962. It was listed as a heritage lighthouse in 2024.

Description: White pyramidal tower

Location: Rocky Point

Directions: From Rocky Point, head south on PE-19 W for 1.4 km and turn left onto Blockhouse Rd where the lighthouse is 1.4 km

Coordinates: 46°11'26.2"N 63°07'45.8"W

Opened: 1876

Automated: 1962

Deactivated: Active

Height: 13 meters, 42 feet

Focal Height: 18 meters, 60 feet

Signal: White flash every seconds

Foghorn signal: N/A

Visitor Access: Grounds open, tower closed

Brighton Beach Range Lighthouses

The original Brighton Beach Range Lights opened in 1889 and were fixed-red from reflector lanterns atop masts. They were replaced by skeleton towers in 18923. The rear tower was destroyed by a gale on October 11, 1900 and a replacement by fire in 1930. The current Brighton Beach Rear Range Lighthouse was erected on in 1968 by Williams, Murphy and MacLeod.

Front range

Description: Square pyramidal tower

Location: Charlottetown

Directions: 160 York Ln
                Charlottetown

Coordinates: 46°13'50.6"N 63°08'51.3"W

Opened: 1890

Automated: 1952

Deactivated: Active

Height: 11 meters, 35 feet

Focal Height: 12 meters, 36 feet

Signal: Fixed yellow

Foghorn Signal: N/A

Visitor Access: Grounds open, tower closed

Rear Range (Image above)

Description: Hexagonal tower flaring

Location: Charlottetown

Directions: 64 Queen Elizabeth Dr,
                Charlottetown

Coordinates: 46°14'02.6"N 63°08'58.7"W

Opened: 1969

Automated: 1952

Deactivated: Active

Height: 18 meters, 60 feet

Focal Height: 27 meters, 87 feet

Signal: Fixed yellow

Foghorn Signal: N/A

Visitor Access: Grounds open, tower closed

Brush Wharf Range Rear Lighthouse

Brush Wharf, is found on the south side of the Orwell River. Ships entering the river would use the Brush Wharf Range Lights to travel to the wharf. The Brush Wharf Front Range Lighthouse was lost to a fire in 1947, and the range was discontinued. The Brush Wharf Rear Range Light has been moved to private property nearby.

Description: Square pyramidal wood tower

Location: Orwell Cove

Directions: From Orwell Cove, head NE on New Cove Rd for 500 m and turn left onto Brush Wharf Rd. After 350 m. turn right onto Orwell Cove Rd and the site is 200 m.

Coordinates: 46°08'32.7"N 62°51'38.1"W

Opened: 1898

Automated: 1947

Deactivated: 1950

Height: 14 meters, 14 feet

Focal Height: 8.5 meters, 28 feet

Signal: Fixed Green

Foghorn signal: N/A

Visitor Access: Closed

Cape Bear Lighthouse

The Cape Bear Lighthouse was erected in 1881 by John Whalen as an aid to local fisherman. In 1947 and 2014, the lighthouse was moved due to erosion of the bank. A Marconi Wireless Telegraph Station was built next to the Cape Bear Lighthouse in 1905, and in 1912 it received the initial distress call from the Titanic. In 1998 the tower was restored and became part of the Marconi Museum exhibit.

Description: White, square pyramidal wooden tower

Location: Beach Point

Directions: From Murray Harbour, head NE on Cape Bear Rd/PE-18 W for 1.9 km and turn left onto Black Brook Rd and the site is 0.5 km.

Coordinates: 46°00'13.0"N 62°27'28.4"W

Opened: 1881

Automated: 1959

Deactivated: 2011

Height: 12 meters, 40 feet

Focal Height: 23 meters, 74 feet

Signal: Yellow flash every 6 seconds

Foghorn Signal: N/A

Visitor Access: Grounds open, tower open in season

Cape Egmont Lighthouse

The Cape Egmont Lighthouse was built by Laurent Perry and opened in 1884. The lighting was upgraded to a 4th order Fresnel in 1906. The keeper's dwelling was removed when the light became automated in 1959. Due to erosion, the tower was moved inland in 2000. The site was designated a Provincial Designated Heritage Place in 2013.

Description: White, square pyramidal wooden tower

Location: Cape Egmont

Directions: From Cape Egmont, head west on PE-11 N for 2.0 km and turn left onto Phare Du Cap Egmont Rd where the site is 750 meters.

Coordinates: 46°24'06.2"N 64°08'05.7"W

Opened: 1884

Automated: 1958

Deactivated: Active

Height: 13 meters, 42 feet

Focal Height: 22 meters, 72 feet

Signal: White flash every 5 seconds

Foghorn Signal: N/A

Visitor Access: Grounds open, tower closed

Cape Tryon Lighthouse

The original Cape Tryon Lighthouse opened in 1905 to guide ships along the northern coast of Prince Edward Island between Richmond Bay and New London. The contractor was B. D. Huntley. In 1906 the lighting was upgraded with a 4th order Fresnel lens. The present tower replaced the original in 1962. The lighthouse was repainted and refurbished in 2018.

Description: White, square pyramidal wooden tower

Location: Park Corner

Directions: From Park Corner, head east on PE-20 N for 3.8 km and turn left onto River Rd. After 1.5 km, turn right onto Cape Rd and in 900 m., right onto Cape Tryon Rd and the site is 1.0 km

Coordinates: 46°32'02.2"N 63°30'21.8"W

Opened: 1969

Automated: 1969

Deactivated: Active

Height: 12 meters, 39 feet

Focal Height: 35 meters, 115 feet

Signal: White flash every 6 seconds

Foghorn signal: N/A

Visitor Access: Grounds open, tower closed

Cardigan River Lighthouse

The original Cardigan River Lighthouse opened in 1883 as a guide to ships into the Cardigan River. The tower was constructed by George Whiteman. The light was deactivated in the early 1980s and sold into private hands. It was moved to its current location at that time.

Description: White, square pyramidal wooden tower

Location: Cardigan

Directions: From Georgetown, head NW on N Royalty Rd for 2.0 km and turn right onto Morrisons Beach Rd. After 800 meters turn left to stay on Morrisons Beach Rd and the site is 100 meters

Coordinates: 46°12'43.2"N 62°32'29.4"W

Opened: 1883

Automated: 1965

Deactivated: 1980

Height: 10 meters, 32 feet

Focal Height: 13 meters, 43 feet

Signal: Fixed Green/white

Foghorn signal: N/A

Visitor Access: Grounds open, tower closed

Cascumpec (Cascumpeque) Lighthouse

The original Cascumpeque Lighthouse was built by Asa McCabe and opened in 1854. As it was found inadequate, a new tower was built by John Smallwood in 1856. However it was found to be beyond repairs by 1874 and a new tower with dwelling was erected in 1876. In 1968 a skeleton tower was erected which was removed in 2005. The image shows this skeleton tower with the former tower behind.

Description: Skeleton tower

Location: Alberton

Directions: Accessible by boat or visible from the marina in Northport

Coordinates: 46°47'55.0"N 64°02'10.0"W

Opened: 1970

Automated: 1970

Deactivated: Active

Height: 18 meters, 59 feet

Focal Height: 18 meters, 60 feet

Signal: 2 white flashes every 10 seconds

Foghorn Signal: Discontinued

Visitor Access: Closed

Covehead Harbour Range Front Lighthouse

In 1879, range lights were erected at the entrance to Covehead Harbour in the form of lights on masts. In 1917 a set of range lights were built by G. L. Gaudin. These lights were automated in 1959. The current Covehead Harbour Lighthouse was established in 1976.

Description: White, square pyramidal wooden tower

Location: Stanhope by the Sea

Directions: From Stanhope by the Sea, head NW on Bayshore Rd/PE-25 N for 3.2 km and turn left onto Gulf Shore Pkwy E and the site is 500 meters

Coordinates: 46°25'48.2"N 63°08'35.3"W

Opened: 1976

Automated: 1976

Deactivated: Active

Height: 8 meters, 27 feet

Focal Height: 10 meters, 33 feet

Signal: White flash every 5 seconds

Foghorn signal: Blast every 30 seconds

Visitor Access: Grounds open, tower closed

Douse Point Range Lights

The Douse Point Range Lights were built in 1899 to guide ships into Orwell Bay. The lights were automated in 1962 and deactivated in 1984. They have been sold to private hands and moved to their current locations.

Front Range

Description: White pyramidal wooden

Location: Murray River

Directions: From Murray River, head SW on PE-4 S for 350 meters and turn left onto Gladstone Rd. After 240 meters the light is on the left

Coordinates: 46°00'47.4"N 62°36'21.6"W

Opened: 1898

Automated: 1962

Deactivated: 1984

Height: 5 meters, 16 feet

Focal Height: 5 meters, 16 feet

Signal: Fixed red

Visitor Access: Closed

Rear Range (Image above)

Description: White pyramidal wooden

Location: Murray River

Directions: From Murray River, head SW on PE-4 S for 350 meters and turn left onto Gladstone Rd. After 240 meters the light is on the left

Coordinates: 46°00'46.4"N 62°36'19.8"W

Opened: 1898

Automated: 1962

Deactivated: 1984

Height: 4 meters, 15 feet

Focal Height: 9 meters, 28 feet

Signal: Fixed green

Visitor Access: Closed

East Point Lighthouse

Numerous requests calling for a lighthouse on East Point were made from shipping interests and one was erected in 1867. William MacDonald was contracted for the project. After ships struck reefs by the site, the tower was moved 488 meters (1,600 feet) closer to the shore in 1885. A fog alarm was added to the station in 1923. The site was listed as a Provincial Designated Heritage Place in 2013 and is still active.

Description: White, octagonal wooden tower

Location: East Point

Directions: From East Point, head SW on Lighthouse Rd off PE-16 for 1.9 km and the site

Coordinates: 46°27'06.3"N 61°58'17.3"W

Opened: 1867

Automated: 1989

Deactivated: Active

Height: 20 meters, 64 feet

Focal Height: 30 meters, 100 feet

Signal: White flash every 5 seconds

Foghorn Signal: 8 second blast every 30 seconds

Visitor Access: Grounds open, tower open mid-June 16 through August

Fish Island Lighthouse

After a catastrophic gale struck in 1852 which devastated the fishing fleet off Prince Edward island, calls were heard for a lighthouse on Fish island. Fishing vessels visiting local harbours were charged duty which raised funds for a station. In 1952 James H. Beckwith was paid to erect a lighthouse on Fish Island. Complaints were soon heard that the light was not adequate and by 1857 a replacement had been erected. In 1877 a new replacement tower was built by Thomas Fahey. A skeleton tower replaced this structure in 1961. There are recent reports that the 1877 tower was no longer to be found on the island.

Description: White, square, pyramidal wooden tower

Location: Malpeque

Directions: From Lower Malpeque, head north on King St toward for 2.5 km and find the site

Coordinates: 46°33'34.2"N 63°42'11.2"W

Opened: 1876

Automated: 1959

Deactivated: 1961

Height: 14 meters, 46 feet

Focal Height: 15 meters, 50 feet

Signal: Fixed white

Foghorn Signal: N/A

Visitor Access: Grounds open, tower closed

Georgetown Range Lights

In 1868 a lighthouse was erected at St Andrews Point to aid ships travelling to the Georgetown Harbour and in 1891 a tower was built to act as a rear range light. The front range light was replaced by a cylindrical tower in 1969. The Georgetown Range Lights were deactivated in 2017.

Front Range

Description: Cylindrical tower

Location: Lower Montague

Directions: From Lower Montague, head on St Andrews Point Rd for 2.6 km

Coordinates: 46°09'47.7"N 62°31'47.0"W

Opened: 1969

Automated: 1969

Deactivated: 2017

Height: 8 meters, 25 feet

Focal Height: 11 meters, 36 feet

Signal: Fixed white

Foghorn signal: N/A

Visitor Access: Closed

Rear Range (Image above)

Description: White, square, pyramidal

Location: Lower Montague

Directions: From Lower Montague, head on St Andrews Point Rd for 2.0 km

Coordinates: 46°09'55.1"N 62°32'13.9"W

Opened: 1891

Automated: 1960

Deactivated: 2017

Height: 13 meters, 43 feet

Focal Height: 19 meters, 62 feet

Signal: Fixed white

Foghorn signal: N/A

Visitor Access: Grounds open, tower closed

Haszard Point Range Lights

Two sets of range lights were erected in 1889 to aid ships travelling into Charlottetown Harbour. The Haszard Range Lights were situated at the southeast harbour entrance. The front range light was moved in 1902 and 1936. Both lights originally had a fixed yellow signal. Both lights are on private property but can be photographed from a public road.

Front Range (Image above)

Description: Red pyramid tower

Location: Stratford

Directions: From Stonington, head NW on Keppoch Rd for 1.1 km and turn right on Lighthouse Ln and the site

Coordinates: 46°11'39.8"N 63°04'25.4"W

Opened: 1889

Automated: 1958

Deactivated: Active

Height: 14 meters, 47 feet

Focal Height: 18 meters, 59 feet

Signal: Fixed yellow

Visitor Access: Closed (Private)

Rear Range

Description: Red pyramid tower

Location: Stratford

Directions: From Stonington, head northeast on Keppoch Rd for 1.1 km and turn left onto Spindrift Ln and the site

Coordinates: 46°11'59.8"N 63°04'15.5"W

Opened: 1889

Automated: 1958

Deactivated: Active

Height: 12 meters, 37 feet

Focal Height: 46 meters, 152 feet

Signal: Fixed yellow

Visitor Access: Closed (Private)

Howard's Cove Lighthouse

The Howards Cove Lighthouse is situated on a hill behind Howards Cove or Seal point. The station was opened in 1960 and the current tower was erected in 1976. It is automated and continues to be active.

Description: White square tower

Location: Cape Wolfe

Directions: From Cape Wolfe, head NW on PE-14 N for 2.1 km and turn left onto Wharf Rd where the site is 0.3 km.

Coordinates: 46°44'24.6"N 64°22'36.3"W

Opened: 1976

Automated: 1976

Deactivated: Active

Height: 6 meters, 19 feet

Focal Height: 14 meters, 47 feet

Signal: White flash every 6 seconds

Foghorn signal: N/A

Visitor Access: Grounds open, tower closed

Indian Head Lighthouse

The Indian Head Lighthouse can be difficult to see and photograph. It was built to aid mariners travelling to the entrance of Summerside Harbour. It can be seen from the Summerside shore or McCallum's Point as per the directions below. In 2019 it received a complete restoration. It is listed as a Provincial Designated Heritage Place.

Description: White octagonal tower

Location: Summerside

Directions: From Bedeque, head north on PE-112 N toward for 8.6 km to the end where you can see the lighthouse at the end of a breakwater

Coordinates: 46°22'45.8"N 63°49'00.8"W

Opened: 1930

Automated: 1961

Deactivated: Active

Height: 13 meters, 42 feet

Focal Height: 14 meters, 46 feet

Signal: White flash every 10 seconds

Foghorn Signal: N/A

Visitor Access: Closed

Leards Range Lights

The Leards Range Lights were erected in 1879 to guide ships into the important harbour at Victoria. Both towers have a vertical red stripe painted on their side facing the sea. The Front range light also served as the Palmer Range Rear Light. The Leards Range Front has been used as the Victoria Seaport Museum during the summer.

Front Range (Image Above)

Description: Square pyramidal wood tower

Location: Victoria

Directions: From Hampton, head SW on Shore Rd for 1.2 km and turn right onto Causeway Rd where the light is 1.7 km

Coordinates: 46°12'50.6"N 63°29'17.8"W

Opened: 1879

Automated: 1960

Deactivated: 2011

Height: 11 meters, 35 feet

Focal Height: 11 meters, 37 feet

Signal: Fixed green

Foghorn Signal: N/A

Visitor Access: Closed

Rear Range

Description: Square pyramidal wood tower

Location: Victoria

Directions: From Victoria, head south on Nelson St for 400 meters and find the light

Coordinates: 46°13'15.0"N 63°29'32.0"W

Opened: 1879

Automated: 1960

Deactivated: 2011

Height: 14 meters, 45 feet

Focal Height: 31 meters, 101 feet

Signal: Fixed green

Foghorn Signal: N/A

Visitor Access: Grounds open, tower closed

Little Channel Range Rear Lighthouse

The Little Channel Range Lights were built by Peter Miller in 1872 on the northern side of Conway Inlet between two barrier islands on the northern shore of Prince Edward Island. They were deactivated in 1969 and at that time the rear tower was moved to its present location where it is used for vacation rental.

Description: Square pyramidal wood tower attached to dwelling

Location: Freeland

Directions: From Freeland, head north on Murray Rd for 1.4 km and turn right onto Henderson Ln where the site is 1.3 km

Coordinates: 46°41'17.1"N 63°56'35.1"W

Opened: 1877

Automated: 1947

Deactivated: 1969

Height: 9 meters, 30 feet

Focal Height: 8 meters, 26 feet

Signal: Fixed white

Foghorn Signal: N/A

Visitor Access: Closed

Malpeque Outer Range (Darnley Point Range) Lights

The original Malpeque Outer Range Lights were erected in 1889 consisting of lanterns on masts. They are also known as the Darnley Point Range Lights. They were replaced by the current lighthouses in 1922. They were automated in 1962 and are still active, The Front Light is listed as a Prince Edward Island Historic Place in 2012.

Front Range

Rear Range (Image Above)

Description: White, square pyramidal tower

Location: Malpeque

Directions: From Lower Darnley, head NW on Lower Darnley Rd for 1.0 km and turn right onto Lighthouse Rd and the site is 600 meters

Coordinates: 46°33'51.4"N 63°39'01.0"W

Opened: 1922

Automated: 1962

Deactivated: Active

Height: 8 meters, 25 feet

Focal Height: 14 meters, 45 feet

Signal: Fixed Red

Visitor Access: Closed

Description: White, square pyramidal tower

Location: Malpeque

Directions: From Lower Darnley, head NW on Lower Darnley Rd for 1.1 km and turn right on Sandpiper Ln and find the site

Coordinates: 46°33'42.2"N 63°39'23.5"W

Opened: 1922

Automated: 1962

Deactivated: Active

Height: 8 meters, 25 feet

Focal Height: 22 meters, 72 feet

Signal: Fixed Red

Visitor Access: Closed

Murray Harbour Range Lights

The Murray Harbour Range Lights where built in 1869 by John Chapman and James Penny as an aid to ships entering the harbour. They were considered inadequate and were replaced by the current towers in 1879. The lights were automated in 1963 and are still active.

Front Range (Image above)

Description: White square tower

Location: Beach Point

Directions: From Beach Point, head NW on Cape Bear Rd for 350 meters and turn left onto Beach Rd and the site is 800 meters

Coordinates: 46°01'15.4"N 62°28'41.9"W

Opened: 1879

Automated: 1983

Deactivated: Active

Height: 7 meters, 23 feet

Focal Height: 6 meters, 20 feet

Signal: Fixed red

Visitor Access: Grounds open, tower closed

Rear Range

Description: White pyramid tower

Location: Beach Point

Directions: From Beach Point, head SW on Cape Bear Rd for 750 m and turn right onto Pennys Ln where the site is 0.5 km

Coordinates: 46°00'52.0"N 62°29'34.1"W

Opened: 1879

Automated: 1983

Deactivated: Active

Height: 13 meters, 43 feet

Focal Height: 17 meters, 56 feet

Signal: Fixed red

Visitor Access: Grounds open, tower closed

New London Range Rear Lighthouse

The New London Lighthouse was built in 1876 by George McKenzie. The light in the lantern room was fixed white while a lower window showed a red light which was visible when the ship was properly aligned. The light was listed as a Prince Edward Island Heritage Place in 2012.

Description: White square tower

Location: Park Corner

Directions: From French River, head NW on River Rd for 1.4 km and turn right onto Cape Rd. After 1.5 km, turn right onto Straight Rd and the site

Coordinates: 46°30'37.5"N 63°29'14.2"W

Opened: 1876

Automated: 1958

Deactivated: Active

Height: 10 meters, 34 feet

Focal Height: 13 meters, 44 feet

Signal: Red flash every 4 seconds

Foghorn signal: N/A

Visitor Access: Closed

North Cape Lighthouse

There is a long dangerous reef separating the Gulf of St. Lawrence and Northumberland Strait which led to calls for a lighthouse in the area. In 1865 funds were budgeted for a lighthouse on North Cape and it was completed by John McLellan. In 1951 the lighthouse was moved inland due to an eroding cliff. In 2013 the light was listed as a Provincial Designated Heritage Place.

Description: Octagonal tower

Location: Seacow Pond

Directions: From Anglo Tignish, head north on PE-12 W for 8.9 km to roads end and the site

Coordinates: 47°03'27.6"N 63°59'47.9"W

Opened: 1867

Automated: 1966

Deactivated: Active

Height: 19 meters, 64 feet

Focal Height: 23 meters, 78 feet

Signal: Yellow flash every 5 seconds

Foghorn signal: N/A

Visitor Access: Grounds open, tower closed

North Rustico Harbour Lighthouse

The current North Rustico Harbour Lighthouse was built by by P. Carroll in 1876 but was opened in 1877 due to lighting equipment delays. In a heavy gale in 1899 the tower tipped over. It was moved farther from the shore and repaired. The light was replaced by a skeleton tower in 1973 but reactivated in 1976 after local protests. It is listed as both a Provincial and Federal Historic site.

Description: White square tower

Location: North Rustico

Directions: From North Rustico, head SW on Harbourview Dr for 1.7 km and see the site

Coordinates: 46°27'19.1"N 63°17'31.3"W

Opened: 1899

Automated: 1960

Deactivated: Active (Inactive 1973-76)

Height: 10 meters, 33 feet

Focal Height: 12.5 meters, 41 feet

Signal: Yellow flash every 10 seconds

Foghorn signal: N/A

Visitor Access: Grounds open, tower closed

Northport Rear Range Lighthouse (Former)

Built in 1897 as the Northport Rear Range Lighthouse, was a 22-foot open-framed wooden tower. In 1903, the tower was enclosed. In 1962 a new front range light was erected and the former front range light was changed to a back end light. The former rear range light was sold to private hands and they incorporated into their house.

Description: Square pyramid

Location: Alberton

Directions: From Alberton. head south on Dufferin St for 700 meters. Turn left onto Carrol St and the site is 600 meters. Private, can be viewed from the beach

Coordinates: 46°48'30.0"N 64°03'10.0"W

Opened: 1897

Automated: 1961

Deactivated: 1962

Height: 13 meters, 43 feet

Focal Height: N/A

Signal: Fixed red

Foghorn Signal: N/A

Visitor Access: Private (Can be viewed from the beach)

Northport Range Rear Lighthouse

This is the original front light of the range erected in 1897. It became the rear light in 1962. It had its height increased by 1.8 meters (6 feet) in 1970 giving it is unique profile. The new front range light is on a skeletal tower.

Description: Square pyramid

Location: Northport

Directions: 218 PE-152, Northport

Coordinates: 46°47'38.3"N 64°03'43.7"W

Opened: 1897

Automated: 1961

Deactivated: Active

Height: 12 meters, 39 feet

Focal Height: 13 meters, 42 feet

Signal: Green flash every 4 seconds

Foghorn signal: N/A

Visitor Access: Grounds open, tower closed

Panmure Head Lighthouse

The Panmure Head Lighthouse was built by Peter Stewart in 1853 to aid captains in entering Georgetown Harbour and avoiding Bear Reef. It is Prince Edward Island's first wooden lighthouse. A 4th order Fresnel lens and fog-alarm building were added in 1908. It was automated in 1985 and continues to be active.

Description: White octagonal tower

Location: Gaspereaux

Directions: From Gaspereaux, head north on Chemin Panmure Island for 4.4 km and find the site

Coordinates: 46°08'37.5"N 62°27'59.9"W

Opened: 1853

Automated: 1985

Deactivated: Active

Height: 18.5 meters, 61 feet

Focal Height: 25 meters, 82 feet

Signal: White flash every 4 seconds

Foghorn signal: Fog alarm building added 1908

Visitor Access: Grounds open, tower open in the summer

Point Prim Lighthouse

The Point Prim Lighthouse is the oldest lighthouse in Prince Edward Island, having been opened in 1845. It was built by Richard Walsh and is an aid to ships travelling to Charlotttetown Harbour. The lighting was upgraded to a 4th order Fresnel lens in 1909. The lighthouse was recognized as a Provincial Designated Heritage Place in 2013.

Description: White cylindrical tower

Location: Point Prim

Directions: From Point Prim, head west on Point Prim Rd for 2.4 km and see the site

Coordinates: 46°03'01.3"N 63°02'18.4"W

Opened: 1845

Automated: 1969

Deactivated: Active

Height: 18.5 meters, 61 feet

Focal Height: 21 meters, 69 feet

Signal: White flash every 5 seconds

Foghorn signal: N/A

Visitor Access: Grounds open, tower open from mid-June through September. Admission

Port Borden Pier Lighthouse

The Port Borden Pier Lighthouse was placed at the outer end of the ferry pier in 1976. It remains active and can be viewed and photographed from the Borden-Carleton waterfront.

Description: White square tower

Location: Port Borden

Directions: From Port Borden, head SW on Borden Ave for 800 meters and find site on breakwater

Coordinates: 46°14'46.6"N 63°42'02.2"W

Opened: 1976

Automated: 1976

Deactivated: Active

Height: 9 meters, 28 feet

Focal Height: 10 meters, 33 feet

Signal: Green flash every 4 seconds

Foghorn signal: N/A

Visitor Access: Closed

Port Borden Range Lights

The Port Borden Range Lights were built in 1918 to guide ferries into the Port Borden Terminal. In 1923 and in 1955 the range lights were moved as the approach to the ferry dock was changed. When the Confederation Bridge was opened in 1997, the lights were deactivated. The Rear Range tower has become part of the Borden-Carleton Marine/Rail Historical Park.

Front Range

Description: White, square pyramidal

Location: Port Borden

Directions: From Borden-Carleton, head south on Belvedere Ave from Main St for 300 meters and the light

Coordinates: 46°15'00.6"N 63°41'39.3"W

Opened: 1918

Automated: 1957

Deactivated: 1997

Height: 6 meters, 22 feet

Focal Height: N/A

Signal: Yellow fixed

Foghorn Signal: N/A

Visitor Access: Closed

Rear Range (Image above)

Description: White, square pyramidal

Location: Port Borden

Directions: From Borden-Carleton, head west on Borden Ave for 450 m and the light

Coordinates: 46°14'59.2"N 63°42'18.6"W

Opened: 1918

Automated: 1957

Deactivated: 1997

Height: 12 meters, 35 feet

Focal Height: N/A

Signal: Yellow fixed

Foghorn Signal: N/A

Visitor Access: Grounds open, tower closed

Seacow Head Lighthouse

The Seacow Head Lighthouse was built in 1864 by David McFarlane and John Rankin, one of five pre-Confederation lighthouses in Prince Edward Island. The lighthouse was relocated in 1979 to avoid erosion. The lighthouse appeared in several episodes of the television series Road to Avonlea. It was listed as a Prince Edward Island Heritage Place in 2003.

Description: White octagonal tower

Location: Fernwood

Directions: From Fernwood, head SW on Fernwood Rd for 800 meters and turn left onto Sea Cow Head Rd. After 900 meters turn right on Lighthouse Rd and the site

Coordinates: 46°18'57.8"N 63°48'38.1"W

Opened: 1864

Automated: 1959

Deactivated: Active

Height: 118 meters, 60 feet

Focal Height: 27 meters, 88 feet

Signal: 2 white flashes every 10 seconds

Foghorn signal: N/A

Visitor Access: Grounds open, tower closed

Shipwreck Point Lighthouse

In 1913 the original Shipwreck Point Lighthouse was built by the Anandale Lumber Company for ships entering Naufrage Pond. The present concrete tower, which replaced it in 1967, was erected by Schurman's Limited. It continues to be active.

Description: White octagonal tower

Location: Big Pond

Directions: From Naufrage, head north on Harbour Road for 250 meters and turn right on Lighthouse Rd to find the site

Coordinates: 46°28'10.5"N 62°25'19.3"W

Opened: 1913

Automated: 1966

Deactivated: Active

Height: 13 meters, 44 feet

Focal Height: 26 meters, 84 feet

Signal: White flash every 5 seconds

Foghorn signal: Blast every 30 seconds

Visitor Access: Closed

Souris East Lighthouse

The Souris East Lighthouse was built in 1879 by Peter Alyward as an aid to ships travelling to the Souris River. The lighthouse was relocated closer to the water in 1885 but returned to its original position due to erosion in 1908. The light is active and operates at night only. It was listed as a Prince Edward Island Heritage Place in 2013.

Description: Square white pyramidal tower

Location: Souris

Directions: From Souris, head south on Parkside Ave from PE-2 for 120 meters and turn left onto Breakwater St and the light is 900 meters

Coordinates: 46°20'47.4"N 62°14'50.7"W

Opened: 1879

Automated: 1991

Deactivated: Active

Height: 19.5 meters, 64 feet

Focal Height: 30.5 meters. 100 feet

Signal: White flash every 5 seconds

Foghorn signal: Discontinued in 1999

Visitor Access: Grounds and tower open

St. Peters Harbour Lighthouse

St. Peters Harbour Lighthouse was built in 1888 to aid ships entering St Peters Bay. It became inactive in 2008. St. Peters Harbour Lighthouse was transferred to St. Peters Harbour Lighthouse Society under the Heritage Lighthouse Protection Act in 2017.

Description: Square white pyramidal tower

Location: St. Peters Harbour

Directions: From Bristol, head north on St Peters Harbour Rd for 2.0 km and turn right onto Lighthouse Rd where the light is 1.5 km

Coordinates: 46°26'30.1"N 62°44'50.6"W

Opened: 1881

Automated: 1963

Deactivated: 2008

Height: 10 meters, 34 feet

Focal Height: 10 meters, 33 feet

Signal: White flash every 6 seconds

Foghorn signal: N/A

Visitor Access: Grounds open, tower closed

St. Peter's Island Lighthouse

The St. Peter's Island Lighthouse was built by Joseph Egan in 18821 to aid ships entering Charlottetown Harbour. The lighthouse was relocated from western side of the island to the southern side in 1884. It was deactivated in 1964 but has since been reactivated.

Description: Square white pyramidal tower

Location: St. Peter's Island

Directions: Accessible by boat

Coordinates: 46°07'01.3"N 63°10'49.9"W

Opened: 1881

Automated: 1947

Deactivated: 1964

Height: 11.6 metres, 38 feet

Focal Height: 14.6 metres, 48 feet

Signal: White flash every 6 seconds

Foghorn Signal: N/A

Visitor Access: Grounds open, tower closed

Summerside Outer Range Lights

The Summerside Outer Range Lights are the last set of Range Lights built in Prince Edward Island. The towers are similar square, pyramidal towers which were opened in 1991. They are both active.

Front Range (Image above)

Description: Square white tower

Location: Summerside

Directions: From Summerside, head SW on MacKenzie Dr from PE-11 for 300 meters and find the site

Coordinates: 46°23'43.1"N 63°48'33.8"W

Opened: 1991

Automated: 1991

Deactivated: Active

Height: 9 meters, 30 feet

Focal Height: 9 meters, 31 feet

Signal: Fixed red

Foghorn Signal: N/A

Visitor Access: Grounds open, tower closed

Rear Range

Description: Square white tower

Location: Summerside

Directions: 701 Water St., Summerside

Coordinates: 46°23'53.7"N 63°48'23.7"W

Opened: 1991

Automated: 1991

Deactivated: Active

Height: 10 meters, 33 feet

Focal Height: 15 meters, 49 feet

Signal: Fixed red

Foghorn Signal: N/A

Visitor Access: Grounds open, tower closed

Summerside Range Lights

The Summerside Range Lights were established in 1895 to aid large steamships entering Summerside Harbour. In 1904, the rear tower was enclosed. The front tower was replaced in 1913. It was deactivated in 1961 and was sold in to private hands and can be viewed from public property at its present location.

Front Range

Description: Square skeleton tower

Location: Summerside

Directions: From Lower Bedeque, head NW on Hector Ln/PE-112 S for 4 km to see the site

Coordinates: 46°21'54.3"N 63°48'18.6"W

Opened: 1913

Automated: 1952

Deactivated: 1961

Height: 11.5 meters, 36 feet

Focal Height: N/A

Signal: Fixed green

Visitor Access: Closed

Rear Range (Image above)

Description: White, square pyramidal

Location: Summerside

Directions: From Summerside, head east on toward King St for 1.0 km and turn right on Glovers Shore Rd and see the site

Coordinates: 46°23'23.4"N 63°46'12.6"W

Opened: 1895

Automated: 1952

Deactivated: Active

Height: 20 meters, 66 feet

Focal Height: 24 meters, 81 feet

Signal: Fixed green

Visitor Access: Closed

Warren Cove Range Lights

Originally called the Warren Farm Range Lights, the Warren Cove Range Lights were erected in 1907 as an aid to the ships entering Charlottetown harbour. The lights are on the grounds of the Fort Amherst/Port La Joye National Historic Site. In 2008 the Coast Guard replaced the siding on both range lights.

Front Range

Description: White, square pyramidal

Location: Rocky Point

Directions: From Rocky Point, head SW on PE-19 W for 1.4 km and turn left onto Blockhouse Rd. In 350 meters turn left onto Hache Gallant Dr and take the trail to the site

Coordinates: 46°11'56.4"N 63°08'17.8"W

Opened: 1907

Automated: 1957

Deactivated: Active

Height: 11 meters, 36 feet

Focal Height: 17 meters, 56 feet

Signal: Fixed yellow

Visitor Access: Grounds open, tower closed

Rear Range (Image above)

Description: White, square pyramidal

Location: Rocky Point

Directions: From Rocky Point, head east on Rocky Point Rd for 400 m and turn right on Cottage Rd for 0.9 km and take trail to site

Coordinates: 46°11'46.3"N 63°08'22.6"W

Opened: 1907

Automated: 1957

Deactivated: Active

Height: 7.7 meters, 25 feet

Focal Height: 23 meters, 75 feet

Signal: Fixed yellow

Visitor Access: Grounds open, tower closed

West Point Lighthouse

The West Point Lighthouse was erected in 1876, the first lighthouse after Prince Edward Island entered Confederation. It is the tallest lighthouse in PEI. It initially had red bands but these were changed to black in 1915. The first keeper was William MacDonald who did the job for 50 years. West Point Lighthouse was listed as a Prince Edward Island Heritage Place in 2012.

Description: White, square pyramidal

Location: West Point

Directions: From West Point, head west on PE-14 N for 650 m and turn left onto Cedar Dunes Park Rd. And after 1.4 km you will see the site

Coordinates: 46°37'13.2"N 64°23'11.8"W

Opened: 1875

Automated: 1963

Deactivated: Active

Height: 20 meters, 67 feet

Focal Height: 20 meters, 67 feet

Signal: White flash every 12 seconds

Foghorn Signal: N/A

Visitor Access: Open

Wood Islands Lighthouse

The Canadian Parliament budgeted funds for the Wood Islands Lighthouse and Archibald McKay began the project which was completed by Donald MacMillian in 1876. The original lighting was a 4th order Fresnel lens. A fog horn was added to the site in 1941. The lighthouse was moved 70 meters inland in 2009 due to erosion. Wood Islands Lighthouse was listed as a Prince Edward Island Heritage Place in 2012.

Description: Square pyramidal tower connected to dwelling

Location: Wood Islands

Directions: From Wood Islands, head SW on PE-1 E for 700 m Meters and turn left onto Lighthouse Rd where the site is 1.0 km

Coordinates: 45°56'59.8"N 62°44'46.2"W

Opened: 1876

Automated: 1989

Deactivated: Active

Height: 16 meters, 52 feet

Focal Height: 22 meters, 72 feet

Signal: White flash every 10 seconds

Foghorn Signal: Fog alarm (Discontinued in 1998)

Visitor Access: Grounds open, tower open in season

Wood Islands Range Lights

The Wood Islands Range Lights were established in 1902 as an aid to ships travelling to Wood Island Harbour. The project was supervised by Milton Walsh. The range was deactivated in 2007 and in 2013 the lighthouses were relocated to a position close to the Wood Islands Lighthouse.

Front Range

Description: White, square pyramidal

Location: Wood Islands

Directions: From Wood Islands, head SW on PE-1 E for 700 m Meters and turn left onto Lighthouse Rd where the site is 1.0 km

Coordinates: 45°57'01.1"N 62°44'46.1"W

Opened: 1902

Automated: 1963

Deactivated: 2007

Height: 4.6 meters, 15 feet

Focal Height: 7 meters, 23 feet

Signal: Fixed red

Foghorn Signal: Fog alarm added in 1946

Visitor Access: Grounds open, tower closed

Rear Range (Image above)

Description: White, square pyramidal

Location: Wood Islands

Directions: From Wood Islands, head SW on: PE-1 E for 700 m Meters and turn left onto Lighthouse Rd where the site is 1.0 km

Coordinates: 45°57'01.1"N 62°44'46.1"W

Opened: 1902

Automated: 1963

Deactivated: 2007

Height: 9 meters, 29 feet

Focal Height: 11 meters, 37 feet

Signal: Fixed red

Foghorn Signal: Fog alarm added in 1946

Visitor Access: Grounds open, tower closed

Wrights Range Lights

The Wrights Range Lights were established to aid ships travelling into Victoria Harbour in 1894. The towers were replaced by the current ones in 1903. The lights were deactivated in 2011.

Front Range (Image above)

Description: White, square pyramidal

Location: Victoria

Directions: From Victoria, head SW on Victoria Rd for 1.0 km and turn left on Beach Light Rd for 600 meters, then left onto Marion Ann Ln for 1.0 km and the site

Coordinates: 46°12'17.2"N 63°29'45.6"W

Opened: 1903

Automated: 1959

Deactivated: 2011

Height: 3.5 meters, 12 feet

Focal Height: 7 meters, 23 feet

Signal: Red flash every second

Visitor Access: Closed

Rear range

Description: White, square pyramidal

Location: Victoria

Directions: From Victoria, head SW on Victoria Rd for 1.0 km and keep left for 210 meters and the site is 750 m

Coordinates: 46°12'24.1"N 63°30'16.9"W

Opened: 1903

Automated: 1959

Deactivated: 2011

Height: 10 meters feet

Focal Height: 7 meters, 23 feet

Signal: Red flash every 4 seconds

Visitor Access: Closed

Tours

Charlottetown Tour

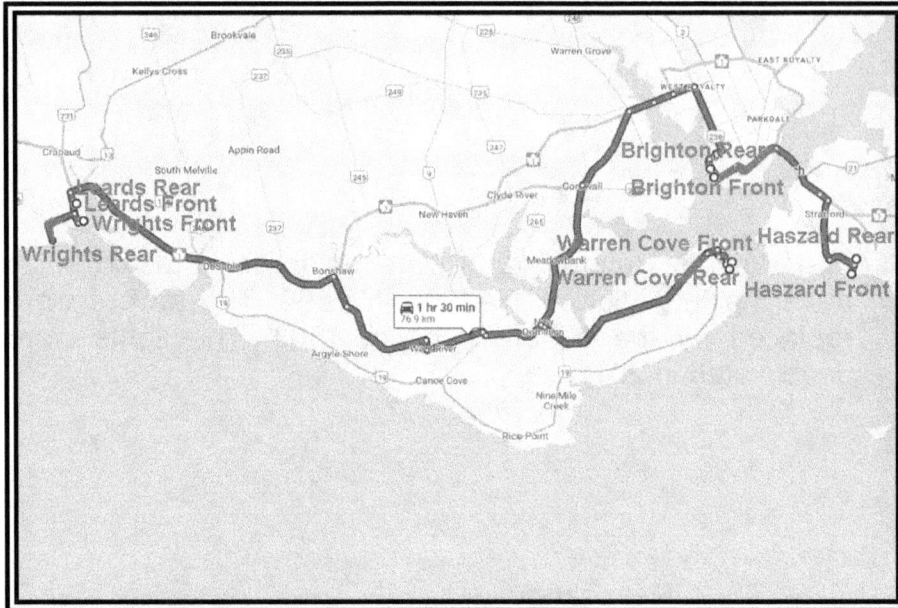

10 lighthouses, 1 hour 30 minutes driving

Haszard Point Front	46°11'39.8"N 63°04'25.4"W
Haszard Point Rear	46°11'59.8"N 63°04'15.5"W
Brighton Beach Front	46°13'50.6"N 63°08'51.3"W
Brighton Beach Rear	46°14'02.6"N 63°08'58.7"W
Warren Cove Front	46°11'56.4"N 63°08'17.8"W
Warren Cove Rear	46°11'46.3"N 63°08'22.6"W
Leards Rear	46°13'15.0"N 63°29'32.0"W
Leards Front	46°12'50.6"N 63°29'17.8"W
Wrights Front	46°12'17.2"N 63°29'45.6"W
Wrights Rear	46°12'24.1"N 63°30'16.9"W

North Central Tour

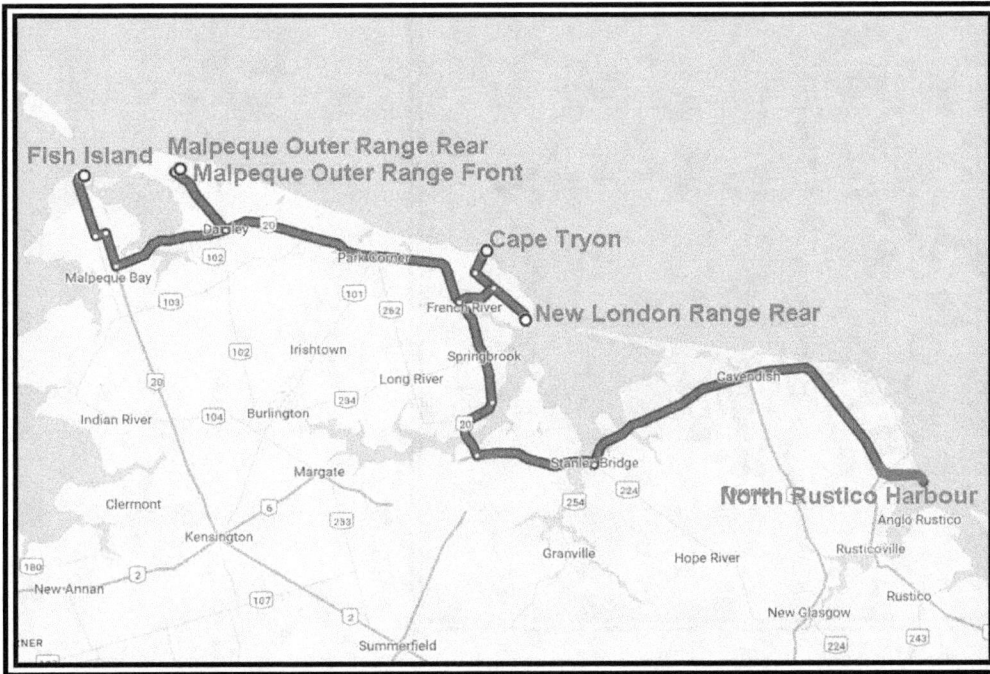

6 lighthouse, 1 hour 15 minutes driving

Fish Island	46°33'34.2"N 63°42'11.2"W
Malpeque Outer Range Rear	46°33'42.2"N 63°39'23.5"W
Malpeque Outer Range Front	46°33'42.2"N 63°39'23.5"W
Cape Tryon	46°32'02.2"N 63°30'21.8"W
New London Range Rear	46°30'37.5"N 63°29'14.2"W
North Rustico Harbour	46°27'19.1"N 63°17'31.3"W

North East Tour

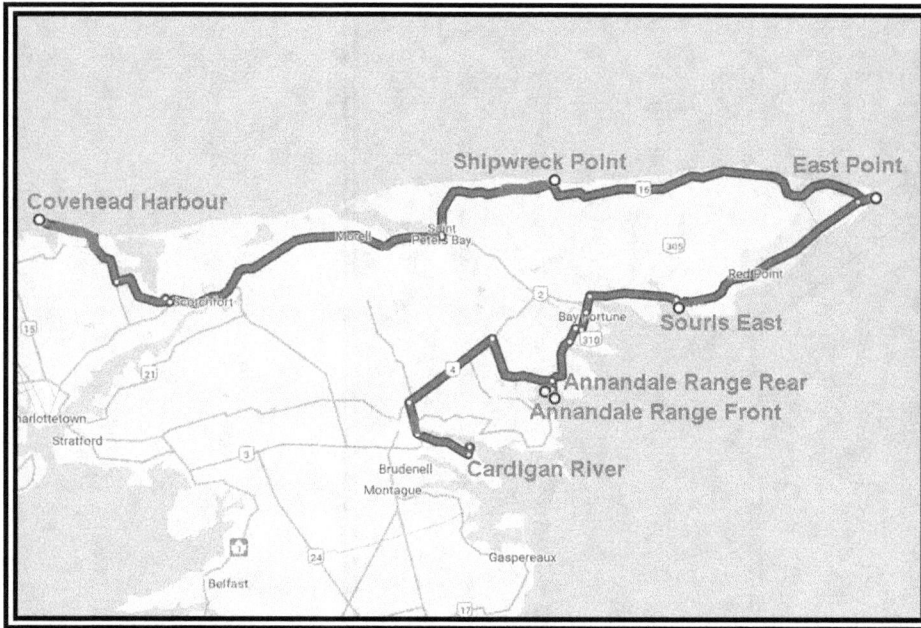

7 Lighthouse, 2 hours 45 minutes driving

Covehead Harbour	46°25'48.2"N 63°08'35.3"W
Shipwreck Point	46°28'10.5"N 62°25'19.3"W
East Point	46°27'06.3"N 61°58'17.3"W
Souris East	46°20'47.4"N 62°14'50.7"W
Annandale Range Rear	46°15'58.0"N 62°26'10.0"W
Annandale Range Front	46°15'33.0"N 62°25'20.0"W
Cardigan River	46°12'43.2"N 62°32'29.4"W

North West Tour

6 lighthouses 1 hour 30 minutes driving

North Cape	47°03'27.6"N 63°59'47.9"W
Big Tignish	46°56'44.8"N 63°59'39.9"W
Northport Range Rear (former)	46°48'30.0"N 64°03'10.0"W
Northport Range Rear	46°47'38.3"N 64°03'43.7"W
West Point	46°37'13.2"N 64°23'11.8"W
Howards Cove	46°44'24.6"N 64°22'36.3"W

South Central Tour

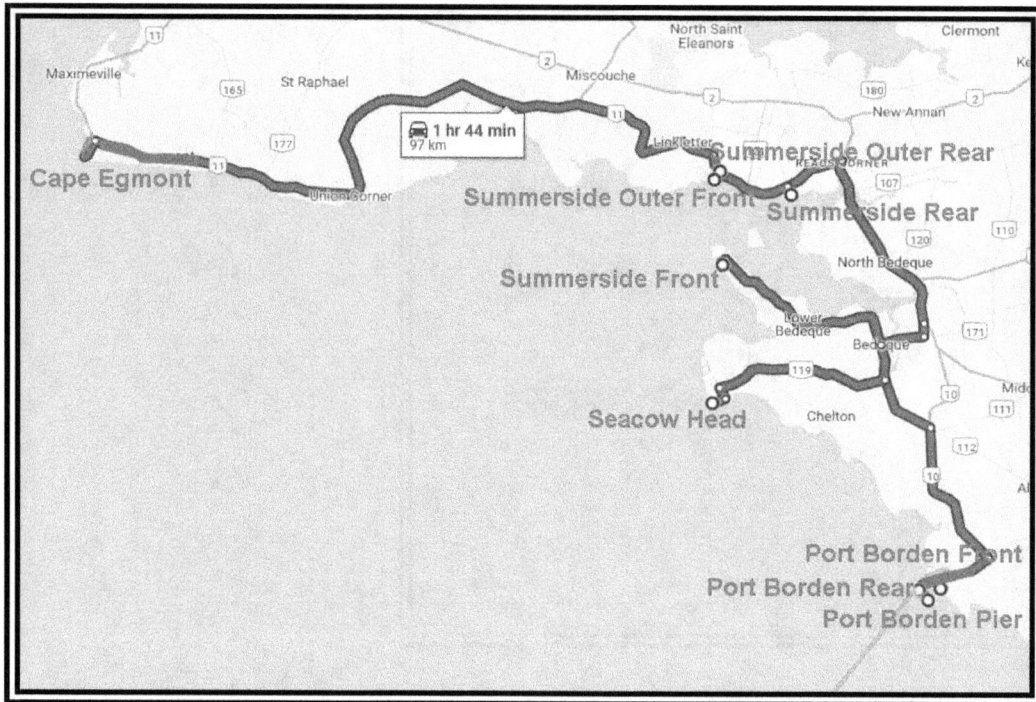

9 lighthouses, 1 hour, 45 minutes

Port Borden Front	46°15'00.6"N 63°41'39.3"W
Port Borden Pier	46°14'46.6"N 63°42'02.2"W
Port Borden Rear	46°14'59.2"N 63°42'18.6"W
Seacow Head	46°18'57.8"N 63°48'38.1"W
Summerside Front	46°21'54.3"N 63°48'18.6"W
Summerside Rear	46°23'23.4"N 63°46'12.6"W
Summerside Outer Front	46°23'43.1"N 63°48'33.8"W
Summerside Outer Rear	46°23'53.7"N 63°48'23.7"W
Cape Egmont	46°24'06.2"N 64°08'05.7"W

South East Tour

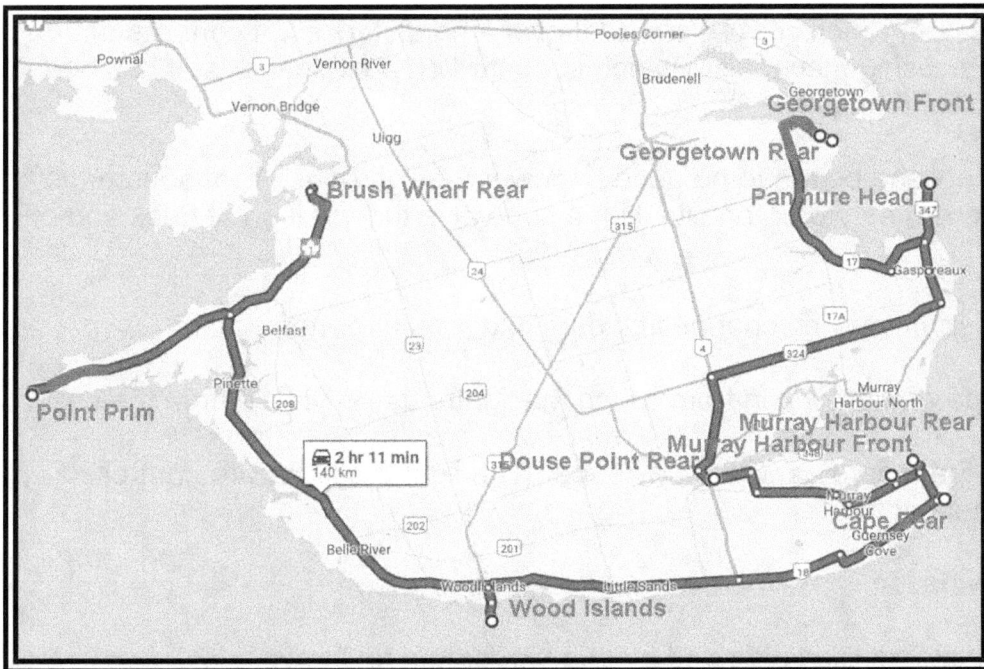

10 lighthouses, 2 hours, 15 minutes driving

Georgetown Range Front	46°09'47.7"N 62°31'47.0"W
Georgetown Range Rear	46°09'55.1"N 62°32'13.9"W
Panmure Head	46°08'37.5"N 62°27'59.9"W
Douse Point Range Rear	46°00'46.4"N 62°36'19.8"W
Murray Harbour Range Rear	46°00'52.0"N 62°29'34.1"W
Murray Harbour Range Front	46°01'15.4"N 62°28'41.9"W
Cape Bear	46°00'13.0"N 62°27'28.4"W
Wood Islands	45°56'59.8"N 62°44'46.2"W
Point Prim	46°03'01.3"N 63°02'18.4"W
Brush Wharf Range Rear	46°08'32.7"N 62°51'38.1"W

Glossary of Lighthouse Terms

Aerobeacon: A lighting system which creates a signal over long distances. It consists of a strong light source with a focusing mechanism which is rotated on a vertical axis. It has been used at airports as well as lighthouses.

Acetylene: After 1910, acetylene began to be used to power the lighthouse light source. It has the advantage that it could be stored on site with a sun valve turning it on at dusk and off at daybreak.

Alternating Light: A light source which changes colours in a regular pattern.

Arc of Visibility: The range of the horizon from which the lighthouse is visible from the sea.

Automated: A lighthouse that operates without a keeper. The light functions are controlled by timers, and light and fog detectors.

Beacon: A fixed aid to navigation.

Bell: A sound signal produced by fixed aids and by sea movement on buoys.

Breakwater: A structure that protects a shore area or harbour by blocking waves.

Bull's-eye Lens: A convex lens used to refract light.

Catwalk: An elevated walkway which allows the keeper to move in the lantern room in towers built in the sea.

Characteristic: The distinct pattern of the flashing light or foghorn blast which allows seamen to distinguish which light station it is coming from.

Chariot: A wheeled assembly at the bottom of a Fresnel lens which is rotated around a circular track.

Clockwork Mechanism: Early lighthouses had a series of gears, pulleys and weights, which had to be wound on a recurring basis by the keepers.

Cottage Style Lighthouse: A lighthouse made up of a keeper's residence with a light on top.

Crib: A base structure filled with stone which acted as the foundation for the structure built on top.

Daymark: A unique colour pattern that identifies a specific lighthouse during the day.

Decommissioned: A lighthouse that has discontinued operating as a aid to navigation.

Diaphone: A sound signal produced by a slotted piston moved by compressed air.

Directional Light: A light which marks the direction to be followed.

Eclipse: The interval between light flashed or foghorn blasts.

Fixed Light: A light shining continuously without periods of eclipse or darkness.

Flashing Light: A light pattern distinguished by periods of eclipse or darkness.

Focal Plane: The path of a beam of light emitted from a lighthouse. The height from the center of the beam to the sea is known as the height of the focal plane.

Fog Detector: A device used to automatically determine conditions which may reduce visibility and the need to start a sound signal.

Fog Signal: An audible device such as a bell or horn that warns seamen during period of fog when the light would be ineffective.

Fresnel Lens: An optic system composed of a convex lens and prisms which concentrate the light beam through a series of prisms. The design was produced by Augustin Fresnel in the 1800s.

Geographic Range: The longest distance the curvature of the earth allows an object of a certain height to be seen.

Isophase Light: A light in which the duration of light and darkness are equal.

Keeper: The person responsible for the maintenance and operation of the lighthouse.

Lamp and Reflector: A lamp and polished mirror used before the invention of more effective optic systems such as the Fresnel lens.

Lantern: A glass covered space at the top of the lighthouse tower, which housed the lighting equipment.

Lens: The glass optical system used to concentrate and direct the light.

Light Sector: The arc over which a light can be seen from the sea.

Lightship: A ship that served as a lighthouse.

Light Station: The lighthouse tower as well as any outbuildings such as the keeper's quarters, fog-signal building, fuel storage building and boathouse.

Nautical Mile: A unit of distance which is the average distance on the Earth's surface represented by one minute of latitude. It is equal to 1.1508 statute miles and mainly used at sea.

Nominal Range: The distance a light can be seen in good weather.

Occulting Light: A light in which the period of light is longer than the period of darkness and in which the intervals of darkness are all equal. Also known as an eclipsing light.

Order: A description of the power of the Fresnel lens ranging from one to seven from stronger to weaker.

Parabolic Reflector: A metal bowl shaped to a parabolic curve which reflects a lamp's light from it's center.

Parapet: A railed walkway which surrounds the lamp room.

Period: The total time for one cycle of the pattern of the light or sound signal.

Pharologist: A person with an interest in lighthouses.

Range Lights: Two lights which form a range provide direction to mariners for safe passage. They are described as the Front and Rear Lighthouses or the Inner and Outer. The front range light is lower than the rear, and when they align, the ship is in the proper position.

Revetment: A bank of stone laid to protect a structure against erosion from waves.

Revolving Light: A flash produced by the rotation of a Fresnel lens.

Riprap: Broken rocks or stone placed to help prevent erosion.

Sector: The portion of the sea lit by a sector light.

Skeleton Tower: Towers consisting of four or more braced feet with a beacon on top. They have little resistance to the wind and waves, and bear up well in a storm.

Solar-powered Optic: Many automated lights are run on solar powered batteries.

Spider Lamp: A brass container holding oil and solid wicks.

Tender: A ship which services lighthouses.

Ventilator: Opening' at the top of a lighthouse tower to provide heat exhaust and air flow within the tower.

Wick Solid: A solid cord which draws fuel to the flame in spider lamps.

Photo Credits

The Photographer's and Explorer's Series

Unless noted, there are Print and eBook editions available for the following.

Birding Guide to Orkney
Guide to Photographing Birds

Maine Lighthouses
Ontario Lighthouses
Orkney and Shetland Lighthouses
Lighthouses of Scotland

Ontario's Old Mills
Ontario Waterfalls

Alabama Covered Bridges (eBook)
Covered bridges of Canada
California Covered Bridges (eBook)
Connecticut Covered Bridges (eBook)
Georgia Covered Bridges (eBook)
Illinois Covered Bridges (eBook)
Indiana Covered Bridges
Iowa Covered Bridges (eBook)
Maine Covered Bridges (eBook)
Massachusetts Covered Bridges (eBook)
Michigan Covered Bridges (eBook)
New Brunswick Covered Bridges
New England Covered Bridges
Covered Bridges of the Mid-Atlantic
Covered Bridges of the South
New Hampshire Covered Bridges
New York Covered Bridges
Ohio's Covered Bridges
Oregon Covered Bridges
Quebec Covered bridges
The Covered Bridges of Kentucky (eBook)
The Covered Bridges of Kentucky and Tennessee
The Covered Bridges of Tennessee (eBook)
Vermont's Covered Bridges
The Covered Bridges of Virginia (eBook)
The Covered Bridges of Virginia and West Virginia
The Covered Bridges of West Virginia (eBook)
Washington Covered Bridges (eBook)
Wisconsin Covered Bridges (eBook)

Index

www.ingramcontent.com/pod-product-compliance
Lightning Source LLC
LaVergne TN
LVHW081337060426
835513LV00014B/1319